COOK JAPANESE

日本料理

COOK JAPANESE

By MASARU DOI

Photographs by
YOSHIKATSU SAEKI

KODANSHA INTERNATIONAL LTD: PUBLISHERS
Tokyo, New York & San Francisco

DISTRIBUTORS:

UNITED STATES: *Kodansha International/USA, Ltd., through Harper & Row, Publishers, Inc., 10 East 53rd Street, New York, New York 10022.* SOUTH AMERICA: *Harper & Row, Publishers, Inc., International Department, 10 East 53rd Street, New York, New York 10022.* CANADA: *Fitzhenry & Whiteside Limited, 150 Lesmill Road, Don Mills, Ontario M3B 2T5.* MEXICO AND CENTRAL AMERICA: *HARLA S. A. de C. V., Apartado 30–546, Mexico 4, D. F.* UNITED KINGDOM: *Phaidon Press Limited, Littlegate House, St. Ebbe's Street, Oxford OX1 1SQ.* EUROPE: *Boxerbooks Inc., Limmatstrasse 111, 8031 Zurich.* AUSTRALIA AND NEW ZEALAND: *Book Wise (Australia) Pty. Ltd., 104–8 Sussex Street, Sydney 2000.* ASIA: *Toppan Company (S) Pte. Ltd., No. 38, Liu Fang Road, Jurong Town, Singapore 2262.*

Published by Kodansha International Ltd., 12-21, Otowa 2-chome, Bunkyo-ku, Tokyo 112 and Kodansha International/USA, Ltd., 10 East 53rd Street, New York, New York 10022 and 44 Montgomery Street, San Francisco, California 94104. Copyright © 1964 by Kodansha International Ltd. All rights reserved. Printed in Japan.

LCC 63–22010
ISBN 0–87011–121–3
JBC 2377–781456 2361

First edition, 1964
Seventh printing, 1980

Table of Contents

Preface

JAPANESE CUISINE is regarded by those familiar with international cookery as probably the most beautiful in the world from the standpoint of appearance and appointments. It is also acknowledged by equally as many as one of the finest when it comes to taste and preparation. Meats, fish, fowl, vegetables, and fruit are served in their most natural state or lightly, crisply, delicately cooked. Seasonings are subtle, minor, but always there.

A glance at the illustrations that follow, and a sampling of the recipes will convince the most skeptical or those who have never ventured into this exotic field. Yet these recipes are simple to follow and all the ingredients or adequate substitutes are available in the United States. In large cities they can be found in shops specializing in imported foods or they can be ordered from one of the mail order food stores such as Oriental Food Store, 1302 Amsterdam Avenue, New York 27, N.Y., whose catalog is a treasure house of Far East foods, cooking, and dining equipment.

While no special techniques are needed to produce these culinary masterpieces, it is suggested that the novice study the process illustrations as well as the photographs. The simple but elegant touches that complete the various dishes can be easily learned and add so much to their beauty. You will note that the choice of plates, bowls, containers, and the arrangement of food itself are most important. Flowers, leaves, vegetable carvings, or folded paper motifs contribute contrasts in color and texture typical of Japanese cookery.

Mr. Doi, on his recent trip to the United States, made a careful study of American tastes and from his enormous collection of Japanese recipes he has selected and presented here those he considers most suitable and most unusual. If portions seem small to you, remember that almost all Japanese meat, fish, and fowl dishes are accompanied by rice. You may follow this custom, or you may substitute noodles or potatoes, or you may simply increase the recipe to meet your requirements. One note of caution: the use of Japanese soy sauce is recommended because non-Oriental soy is more concentrated and saltier. If American soy is used, smaller quantities are suggested. Recipes serve 4 unless indicated.

5

The Author

MASARU DOI, born on the island of Shikoku in 1921, embarked upon his career as a cook at the age of 15 when he entered the Osaka Cooking School where he obtained a degree as a nutritionist. During the war he served in the Japanese Navy as a cook-nutritionist, receiving additional specialized training. In 1953, Mr. Doi established the Kansai Kappo Gakuin, a now famous cooking school from which 45,000 students have been graduated. Besides directing this school which has a current enrollment of 4,500 students and a staff of 47 instructors, he teaches many groups of women's club members, and is one of the most popular instructors of Japanese cookery on television, appearing weekly on a national hookup. He has written extensively in Japanese on cookery and has also had one book published in English. Masaru Doi is an avid fisherman and a former Olympic sprinter. Collaborating with him in producing this authentic and delightful collection of unusual Japanese foods are Yoshikatsu Saeki who is responsible for the magnificent photographs; Masakazu Kuwata who directed the design and art work; and Lucille Evans who gave advice and help in the preparation of the manuscript. Utensils for serving were provided by The Craft Center of Japan in Tokyo.

パーティー

Party Food

SUKIYAKI

THIS IS probably Japan's most famous dish. It is so important in a Japanese home that the father is usually the one to give finishing touches to the flavor. (serves six)

Ingredients
  1 1/2-2 lbs. beef (rib roast or sirloin in 1/8″ slices)
  2 loaves roasted *tofu* cut in 1″ squares
  14 oz. *shirataki*, boiled 1–2 minutes and cut in 2″ lengths
  1 oz. *fu* soaked in water to soften and pressed to drain
  10 stalks leek cut in 2″ lengths aslant
  suet to grease pan
  2/3 lbs. *shungiku*
  warishita (see basic recipe page 127)

Utensils and Equipment
  Large heavy skillet (electric is best for table cooking); *hibachi*; mixing bowls.

Method
  Arrange ingredients decoratively and place at table side. Oil pan thoroughly with piece of suet and heat. Put beef in piece by piece and brown both sides, add other ingredients and *warishita* and cook over medium heat. Serve and eat while cooking, adding ingredients as food is removed. Do not add water if sauce cooks away. Use *saké* and lower heat to avoid overcooking. Add soy sauce and sugar to adjust taste.

Variations
  Substitute meat balls for sliced beef and sliced onions for leeks. Add fresh mushrooms, or watercress. Use fresh eggs (beaten lightly) as a dip, one egg for each guest.

すきやき

SUKIYAKI

SUSHI

THIS ENORMOUSLY popular rice dish is given here in variations suitable for Western taste. (serves six)

Ingredients

    4 cups rice (*see basic recipe page 127*) cooled
    2 cucumbers, 8″ long
    4 oz. smoked salmon, 1/8″ thick
    4 oz. boiled ham, 1/8″ thick
    4 oz. *teriyaki* fish (*see basic recipe page 58*)
    4 tbsps. prepared mustard
    2 tbsps. pickled red ginger, cut in thin strings
    marinade for salmon: 1/2 cup vinegar, 1 1/2 tbsps. sugar, 1/2 tsp. salt

Utensils and Equipment

    Two 8″ square baking pans; wax paper; cutting board.

Method

    Pare cucumbers, rub well with salt, and slice vertically 1/8″ thick. Sprinkle salmon with salt and marinate for 15 minutes. Slice *teriyaki* fish in 1/8″ strips. Place wax paper on bottom of one pan and line with cucumbers. Spread thin layer of mustard over them. Pack 2″ layer of rice firmly on top and, using second pan, press rice down well (*see process illustration*). Let stand 10 minutes. Remove top pan and turn first pan upside down on cutting board, emptying contents. Remove wax paper and cut rice cake into squares 1 1/4″ × 1 1/2″. Serve with strips of ginger. Salmon, ham, and *teriyaki* fish are processed in the same manner.

Variations

    Roast beef, boiled shrimps, or cheese, may be substituted, and mayonnaise may be used in place of mustard.

SUSHI

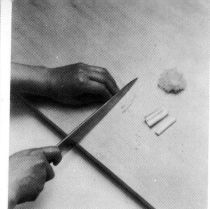

MIZUTAKI

THIS FAVORITE cold weather dish contains delicious chicken bits combined with Chinese cabbage and *tofu*. Using your prettiest casserole, start preparations in the kitchen, and finish cooking over a *hibachi*. (serves six)

Ingredients

2 1/2 lbs. chicken chopped in 1″ squares
1 lb. Chinese cabbage, cut in 1″ width strips
1 loaf *tofu* cut in 1″ blocks
1 bunch watercress cut in 2″ lengths
8 dried mushroom caps softened in water
1 4″ square sheet *dashi konbu*
momiji-oroshi: 10 oz. *daikon*, 3–5 dried red peppers, seeded. Make holes in cut end of *daikon*, insert red peppers, and grate (*see process illustration*).
sarashi-negi: 1 stalk leek, cut in 1″ length, then cut vertically in half and finely shredded (*see process illustration*). Wrap in damp cloth, wash well, and wring.
pon-zu sauce (see basic recipe page 127)

Utensils and Equipment

Large casserole; *hibachi*; grater.

Method

Fill casserole 3/4 full of water and put in *dashi konbu* and 1/3 of chicken. Cook over medium heat until water boils, then add vegetables. Cook over medium heat 5 minutes. Add the rest of the chicken. Place casserole on *hibachi*. Do not overcook. Serve and eat while cooking. Put spoonful of *momiji-oroshi* and pinch of *sarashi-negi* in *pon-zu* sauce and use as dip.

Variations

Add clams or use oysters instead of chicken.

水たき

MIZUTAKI

TEMPURA

HERE IS a new way to prepare *tempura* that makes it the perfect party dish—indoors or out. (serves six)

Ingredients

12 canned sweet chestnuts, drained
3 stalks celery, cut in 1 1/4″ lengths
30 small shrimp, peeled, heads removed, tails left intact
6 bell peppers, cut vertically in half and seeded
1 lb. pork 1/4″ slices cut in 1″ squares
1 lb. beef 1/4″ slices cut in 1″ squares
12 small onions, peeled and halved
1 lb. white meat fish fillet, cut in approximately 1″ pieces
momiji-oroshi (*see basic recipe page 12*)
sarashi-negi (*see basic recipe page 12*)
goma-shio: 2 tbsps. sesame seed mixed with 1/3 cup table salt. Roast sesame seeds in dry skillet over low heat until a few seeds burst.
tempura sauce (*see basic recipe page 127*)
tempura batter (*see basic recipe page 127*)
5-8 cups *tempura* oil (sesame seed oil, vegetable oil)

Utensils and Equipment

Mixing bowl and thick chopsticks for batter; iron tea kettle (or electric deep-fry pan); *hibachi*; 60 bamboo skewers (8″ long).

Method

Arrange all ingredients on platters and place near deep-fry pan. Mix batter carefully and slowly so it does not become gluey. Spear meat, vegetable, or fish pieces with skewers, dip in batter, and deep fry in oil at 350° for 4–5 minutes. Do a few at a time and eat as soon as drained. Put 1 tsp. each *momiji-oroshi* and *sarashi-negi* in *tempura* sauce and use as dip for *tempura* or sprinkle with *goma-shio* to eat. Serve *tempura* with raw vegetables, such as celery, radishes, or cole slaw.

Variations

Use catsup sauce or mayonnaise sauce instead of *tempura* sauce.

14

TEMPURA

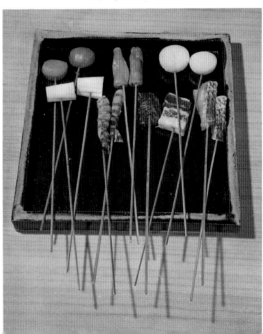

ONIGIRI

THESE ATTRACTIVE-looking rice balls are a favorite picnic dish in Japan and are also popular for evening snacks while watching TV. (serves six)

Ingredients
    6 cups cooked rice (*see basic recipe page 127*)
    2 tbsps. *goma-shio* (*see basic recipe page 14*)
    2 tbsps. *oboro ebi*
    1 sheet *nori* dried over low heat and cut in 1/2″ strips
    3 oz. pickled red ginger, shredded

Utensils and Equipment
    Bowl of salt water to wet hands (3 tsps. salt to 1 cup water).
Method
    Wet hands with salt water and mold hot rice into balls. Oblong or triangular shapes may also be made (*see process illustration*). Sprinkle some with *goma-shio*, press a teaspoon of *oboro ebi* on top of some, and band others with a strip of *nori*. Serve with red pickled ginger. Other variations can be made: press a hole in center and insert broiled salmon or fried fish. These are especially good with *miso* soup.

ONIGIRI

17

TEPPAN-YAKI

AN UNUSUAL mélange for a barbecue: beef, sweet potatoes, shellfish, and green peppers in a delicious combination, completed by zesty sauces for dipping. (serves six)

Ingredients
3/4 lb. beef (tenderloin, sirloin or rib roast) sliced 1/4″ thick
1 large sweet potato sliced in 1/4″ thick
6 large oysters, rinsed in light salt water and replaced in shell
6 bell peppers, stem and seeds removed, sliced vertically in halves
6 prawns, peeled and cleaned
momiji-oroshi (*see basic recipe page 12*)
sarashi-negi (*see basic recipe page 12*)
pon-zu sauce (*see basic recipe page 127*)
catsup sauce: 2 tbsps. Worcestershire sauce, 2 tsps. mustard, 1/2 cup tomato catsup, 2 tsps. lemon juice
vegetable oil for grill

Utensils and Equipment
Grill; mixing bowls; large toothpicks or skewers.
Method
Have ingredients and sauces prepared before you start cooking. Oil griddle and grill food a little at a time as you serve and eat. Dip hot food into sauce of your choice. Do not overcook.
Variations
Chicken, lobster, oysters in season, fresh mushrooms, sliced onions, white meat fillet of fish, can be used. Other delicious sauces: (a) mix together 1 tbsp. mustard, 5 tbsps. soy sauce, 2 tbsps. Worcestershire sauce; (b) *goma-shio* (*see basic recipe page 14*).

鉄板焼き

TEPPAN-YAKI

KAISEKI

A FORMAL Japanese dinner is called *kaiseki ryori*. This menu is an abbreviated form. (serves six)

Zensai (hors d'oeuvres)

Ikura-no-Yuzugama (Salmon Roe in Citron)
Ingredients
    6 tbsps. salmon roe
    6 citron (substitute halves of small limes or lemons)
Method
    Cut off top of citron, remove flesh, and fill with salmon roe. Replace top.

Kuri-no-Shiropu-ni (Chestnuts Cooked in Syrup)
    12 canned chestnuts cooked in syrup.
Method
    Drain and serve.

Takara-yaki Tamago (Egg Omelette) (*see recipe page 36*)

Tai-no Lemon *Oshi* (Sea Bream Pressed with Lemon)
Ingredients
    12 oz. sea bream fillets
    1 cup salt
    1 lemon
    marinade: 1 cup vinegar, 3 tbsps. sugar, 1 tsp. salt, 1 tsp. soy sauce
Method
    Salt sea bream and let stand for 2 hours. Then soak in marinade for 30 minutes. Remove skin and slice to 1/4" thickness. Slice lemon and make sandwich of fish and lemon slices. Cut in two to serve.

Teriyaki Fish (*see page 58*)

Ebi-to-Kyuri-no-Sunomono (Shrimp-Cucumber in Vinegar Sauce)
Ingredients
    6 shrimp, boiled and peeled, leaving tail. Cut into three pieces
    2 cucumbers, 6" long, cut in 3/4" strips
    marinade: 1 cup vinegar, 3 tbsps. sugar, 1 tsp. salt, 1 tsp. soy sauce
Method
    Marinate shrimp for 30 minutes. Salt cucumbers and dip into marinade before serving.

Nasu-no-Dengaku (Eggplant with *Miso* Paste)
Ingredients
    1/2 small eggplant sliced in 1" pieces (3 pieces for each person)
    3 tbsps. vegetable oil
    miso paste: 1/2 cup *miso*, 4 tbsps. sugar, 2 tbsps. *saké*
    1 tsp. white sesame seeds
    12 small green chili peppers or 1 bell pepper, cut in 12 pieces, seeded
    dash salt, butter
Method
    Heat oil and sauté eggplant slices over medium heat to brown both sides. Lower heat and cook for 7–8 minutes with cover. Cook *miso* paste over low heat mixing well for 3–4 minutes. Sprinkle salt over green peppers and sauté in butter. Serve eggplant applying coat of *miso* paste and garnish with white sesame seeds.

KAISEKI

21

YAKITORI

A DELIGHTFUL replacement for canapes, especially for an outdoor cocktail party. If bamboo server is not available, use exotic Oriental bowls. (serves six)

Ingredients
    1 1/2 lbs. chicken meat diced in 3/4″ squares
    1/2 lb. chicken livers washed in salt water and diced in 3/4″ squares
    3 tbsps. vegetable oil
    teriyaki sauce: 1/3 cup soy sauce, 5 tbsps. sugar, 2 tbsps. *mirin*
    1 cup cocktail sauce: Your favorite recipe, or ready-made
    1/2 cup *goma-shio* (*see basic recipe page 14*)
    10 stalks celery, dressed
    1 carrot, cut into thin sticks
    20 green onions, dressed
    1/2 cup cabbage cole slaw
    3 cucumbers, quartered vertically

Utensils and Equipment
    24 10″ bamboo skewers; skillet; *hibachi* or brazier; bamboo poles split through middle.
Method
Heat oil in skillet and sauté chicken over high heat for 6–7 minutes. Then pour *teriyaki* sauce in pan and cook for another 3–4 minutes shaking skillet. Repeat the same process for chicken livers. Place 5–6 pieces chicken and livers alternately on bamboo skewers. Reheat over charcoal before serving. Crisp vegetables in ice water just prior to serving. Arrange bamboo poles as shown in illustration with cocktail sauce, *goma-shio*, vegetables, and water to serve as finger bowl.

YAKITORI

23

Appetizers 前菜

LEMON-IKURA

HORS D'OEUVRES in the Japanese manner are as colorful as they are tasty. (serves six)

Ingredients
    6 tbsps. salmon roe
    6 slices lemon

Method
    Mold 1 tablespoon salmon roe on each slice of lemon and serve well chilled.

HANAYASAI

Ingredients
    1 small head of cauliflower (washed in 5 cups of water to which 2 tsps. salt have been added)
    2 tsps. vinegar
    6 tbsps. mayonnaise

Method
    Put vinegar in boiling water, add cauliflower and cook for 10 minutes in a saucepan covered by smaller size lid. Cool and break into small pieces. Place on platter and serve with mayonnaise.

IGA-AGE

FRIED CHESTNUTS in "thorns" are not only delicious to eat but most attractive to the eye. (serves six)

Ingredients
    12 chestnuts (sweet cooked canned)
    1/4 lb. *somen*, broken in 3/4" pieces
    1/2 cup *tempura* batter (*see basic recipe page 127*)
    flour
    vegetable oil

Utensils
    Mixing bowl; skillet; platter for *somen*.
Method
    Flour chestnuts and dip in batter. Roll in *somen*, fry in hot oil (350°) until brown. Remove, drain on absorbent paper and serve.
Variations
    Substitute hard-boiled quail eggs, shrimp, or chicken balls for chestnuts.

IGA-AGE
LEMON-IKURA   HANAYASAI

27

BAIKA-MUSHI

THE AMAZINGLY attractive results from this easy-to-do recipe will put it high on your list of party surprise snacks. (serves six)

Ingredients
  5 frankfurters, boiled and cut in halves
  1 hard-boiled egg sieved and mixed well with:
  2 tbsps. flour
  1 tsp. sugar
  1/8 tsp. salt

Utensils and Equipment
  Two 4″ by 8″ squares of tin foil; steam cooker.
Method
  Dampen the foil and hold in hand. Arrange three strips of frankfurter with middle piece slightly lower (*see process illustration*) and pack in half of egg mixture to fill opening. Then place two pieces of frankfurter on top and wrap firmly. Repeat with other half of ingredients. Place in steam cooker for 7–8 minutes. Cool and cut into 3/4 inch pieces to serve.

Recipes for other hors d'oeuvres in the color photograph are listed on page 123.

BAIKA-MUSHI   MEIGETSU-TAMAGO   TSUKE-YAKI
NAMBAN-ZUKE   TOFU-DENGAKU

玉子

Egg Dishes

TAKARA-MUSHI

A VERY NEW WAY to use pumpkin—stuffed with chicken, eggs, shrimp, peas, and mushrooms—and a colorful dish to serve.

Ingredients
    2 pumpkins (2 lbs. each)
    4 tsps. salt
    2 tbsps. *saké*
    10 dried mushroom caps softened in water, sliced fine
    7 oz. chicken meat diced in 1/4″ pieces
    5 eggs beaten lightly
    7 oz. small shrimp, peeled
    1/4 cup green peas
    1 tbsp. salt
    1 tbsp. soy sauce
    1 1/2 tbsps. sugar
    2 tbsps. *saké*

Utensils and Equipment
    Steam cooker; mixing bowl.

Method
Cut tops off pumpkins, remove seeds, and peel skin in several places. Sprinkle with salt and pour in *saké*. Let stand for 10 minutes. Steam over high heat for 7–8 minutes. Mix mushrooms, chicken, shrimp, and green peas with egg, add salt, soy sauce, sugar and *saké* and pour mixture into pumpkin. Steam over medium heat for 20–25 minutes. (The cooked pumpkin will crack if steamed over strong heat.) Quarter pumpkin when serving.

TAKARA-MUSHI

CHAWAN-MUSHI

A TYPICAL Japanese egg dish served with fried or broiled meat, and a favorite of children.

Ingredients
4 eggs
soup stock (4 times the quantity of eggs), cooled (*see basic recipe page 127*)
2/3 tsp. salt
1 tsp. *mirin*
3 oz. chicken diced and sprinkled with 1 tsp. soy and let stand for 4–5 minutes
1 oz. white meat fish, cut in 4 slices and sprinkled with salt
4 small shrimp, peeled and cleaned
4 small dried mushroom caps, softened in water
1 oz. string beans slightly boiled and sliced thin

Utensils and Equipment
4 individual casseroles with lids; steam cooker; cloth to strain; mixing bowls.

Method
Beat eggs lightly. Add salt, and *mirin* to soup stock and mix with egg. Then strain and pour in casseroles with chicken, shrimp, fish and mushrooms. Remove foam and place in steam cooker with casserole lids slightly ajar and steam over medium heat for 25 minutes. Garnish with string beans just before removing from cooker. Serve hot.

Variations
Use about 1/4 less soup stock for firmer consistency. Use cooked noodles or *tofu* in egg mixture.

茶わん蒸し

CHAWAN-MUSHI

35

IRI-TAMAGO

Scrambled eggs with mushroom, cabbage, and shrimp make an easy Sunday supper.

Ingredients
  7 oz. small shrimp, peeled and cleaned
  4 dried mushroom caps softened in water and quartered
  10 oz. cabbage washed and cut in 1″ squares
  4 eggs beaten and mixed with 2 tbsps. soup stock (*see basic recipe page 127*), 2 tsps. sugar, 1 tsp. salt, 1 1/2 tsps. soy, 1 1/2 tsps. *mirin*
  1 tbsp. vegetable oil

Utensils and Equipment
  Large skillet; chopsticks or fork to scramble eggs.
Method
  Sauté shrimps and mushrooms in vegetable oil over strong heat for 2–3 minutes. Add cabbage and cook few moments longer. Lower heat and pour in egg mixture. Scramble lightly until set.
Variations
  Use ham or sausage instead of shrimp, green peas instead of cabbage.

TAKARA-YAKI

A SIMPLE OMELETTE using crab, *tofu*, mushrooms, and green peas which, in Japan, is served at breakfast or with meat or fish dishes. For Westerners an interesting brunch or supper dish.

Ingredients
  10 oz. *tofu* well drained and crushed
  3 dried mushroom caps, softened in water and sliced fine
  6 oz. canned crabmeat, gristle-free and well minced
  3 eggs beaten well
  1 tsp. *mirin*
  1/3 tsp. soy sauce
  1 tsp. flour
  1 tbsp. canned green peas (substitute frozen or fresh peas lightly boiled)
  1 tbsp. vegetable oil

Utensils and Equipment
  Mixing bowl; skillet or electric frying pan with cover.
Method
  Mix *tofu*, mushroom, crabmeat, eggs, *mirin*, soy sauce, flour, and green peas. Heat oil and pour half mixture into skillet, cover and cook over low heat until set, about 15 minutes. Repeat process with other half of mixture. Slice into pieces 1″ × 2″. Serve hot with soy sauce.
Variations
  Use shrimp, ham, or minced chicken instead of crabmeat.

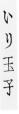

いり玉子

IRI-TAMAGO

賓焼き

TAKARA-YAKI

37

TAMAGO-DOFU

A CUSTARD-LIKE egg dish served hot in winter and cold in summer. Good with *tempura, teriyaki* fish, or as an hors d'oeuvre.

Ingredients

6 eggs; soup stock equivalent in volume to eggs (*see basic recipe page 127*)
2/3 tsp. salt
1 tsp. *mirin* (substitute 1 tsp. *saké* plus 1/2 tsp. sugar)
2/3 tsp. *usukuchi* (light-colored) soy. (If light colored soy is not available, use regular soy and add 1/5 tsp. salt)
Sauce: 1 cup soup stock, 1/4 tsp. salt, 2–3 drops soy
2 slices lemon or lime, cut in quarters

Utensils and Equipment

4 small molds with covers; cloth to sieve; steam cooker; mixing bowl.

Method

Mix eggs lightly with soup stock and add salt, *mirin*, and light-colored soy sauce. Lay cloth in molds, pour in egg mixture and strain slowly by twisting four ends of cloth and squeezing. Remove foam, cover molds with cloth (leave lids of mold slightly ajar). Place in steam cooker and steam in medium heat for 25 minutes. Unmold and cut in halves. Serve hot or cold, covered with sauce and garnished with sliced lemon or lime. Egg can be mixed with soup stock up to 2 1/2 times the quantity of eggs. Do not steam over high fire.

Variations

Use minced dried red shrimp and green peas for added color. Thin slices of shrimp may be used in soup.

玉子どうふ

TAMAGO-DOFU

NISHIKI-TAMAGO

AN EGG DISH which may be served as a dessert or at tea time as a special treat. Its name means " brocade egg."

Ingredients
    10 hard-boiled eggs (12–13 minutes)
    15 tbsps. sugar
    1/8 tsp. salt

Utensils and Equipment
    Sieve; covered mold or baking pan; steam cooker.
Method
    Sieve whites and yolks of eggs separately. Mix whites with 6 tbsps. of sugar and 1/8 tsp. of salt. Mix yolk with 9 tbsps. of sugar. Place the white mixture in mold and top with yolk mixture, pressing lightly. Cover and steam over high heat 7–8 minutes. Cool and cut in 1″ –1 1/2″ squares to serve.
Variations
    Use baking pan and tin foil if mold not available. Heat in moderate oven for 10 minutes.

40

錦玉子

NISHIKI-TAMAGO

Rice Dishes

KAYAKU-GOHAN

RICE COOKED with chicken and other ingredients and flavored with soy sauce and *saké* is good for a buffet supper. *Kamameshi*, which is the same type of rice dish, is a popular specialty at Japanese restaurants.

Ingredients
 4 cups rice, washed and drained
 4 oz. chicken diced in 1/4″ squares
 marinade for chicken: 1/3 cup soy sauce, 2 tbsps. *saké*
 1 carrot diced in 1/8″ squares
 1 piece *abura age* cut in 1/4″ squares (substitute 1 tbsp. butter)
 3 tbsps. green peas. Pour boiling water over peas and drain.

Utensils and Equipment
 Rice cooker; bowl for marinade.
Method
 Marinate chicken for 4–5 minutes. Put rice and same amount of water in cooker, add all ingredients including marinade, stir and cook. When rice is cooked, mix ingredients lightly and serve. Rice with salt and soy sauce mixtures tends to cook faster, therefore shorten the medium heat cooking to 4–5 minutes and the low heat to 12–13 minutes.

Variations
 Use clams, fish, or meat to suit taste.

ASARI-GOHAN

RICE, CLAMS and leek are combined in an interesting dish.

Ingredients
 10 oz. small clams soaked in 5 cups water and 2 tsps. salt for 4–5 hours, or 8 oz. canned clams
 1 leek cut in 1/2″ pieces—use white part only
 marinade: 2/3 tsp. salt, 1 tbsp. soy sauce, 2 tbsps. *saké*
 4 cups rice
 1 sheet *nori*

Utensils and Equipment
 Bowl; saucepan to boil clams; strainer; rice cooker; scissors.
Method
 Clean fresh clams and boil in 5 1/2 cups water until clams open. Shell clams. Strain boiled water and save to cook rice. Marinate clams and leek for 10 minutes. Cook rice with 4.8 cups of water used to boil clams. At boiling point, add clams, leek, and marinade. Cook until rice is done. Put *nori* in warm oven to remove dampness (it burns easily) and cut in fine strips with scissors. Mix rice lightly to serve and garnish with *nori*.
Variations
 Substitute large clams, oysters, or scallops for small clams.

KAYAKU-GOHAN   ASARI-GOHAN

45

CHIRASHI-ZUSHI

For BIRTHDAYS or holidays this vinegared rice is a special treat and popular with children.

Ingredients
4 cups rice (*see basic recipe page 127*)
vinegar mixture: 2/5 cups vinegar, 4 tbsps. sugar, 1 1/2 tbsps. salt
6 dried mushroom caps, softened in water, sliced thin
sauce for cooking mushroom: 2 tbsps. sugar, 1 tbsp. *saké*, 3 tbsps. soy sauce
7 oz. small boiled shrimp
marinade for shrimp: 3 tbsps. vinegar, 1/2 tbsps. sugar, 1/3 tsp. salt
2 hard-boiled eggs, sieve yolk and chop whites fine
1 handful cooked string beans, sliced thinly aslant

Utensils and Equipment
Rice cooker; 2 mixing bowls; 4 saucepans; large enameled pan and spatula to mix cooked rice; fan or electric fan to cool rice when mixing.

Method
Place vinegar mixture over low heat to melt sugar and salt. Put cooked rice in enameled pan, use spatula to mix rice, constantly turning and cutting while slowly pouring in vinegar mixture. Use fan to cool rice while mixing. Cook mushrooms over low heat, barely covered with water used for softening for 5–6 minutes. Add sugar, *saké*, and soy sauce and cook for 3–4 minutes. Marinate cooked shrimps 4–5 minutes. Mix rice with mushrooms and shrimp. Garnish with sliced string beans, egg yolk and whites.

FUKUSA-ZUSHI

A nutritious and filling variation of *chirashi-zushi.*

Ingredients
4 cups *chirashi-zushi*
4 eggs well-beaten with 1/2 tsp. salt
7 oz. boiled shrimp peeled, and chopped fine
3 tbsps. sugar
1/3 tsp. salt
red food coloring; enough to color shrimp
1 tbsp. vegetable oil

Utensils and Equipment
Skillet; chopsticks; saucepan; damp cloth.

Method
Heat oil and pour in thin layer of beaten eggs. Keep heat low to medium in order to maintain yellow color of egg. When surface begins to dry, use chopsticks to loosen edges and then insert halfway to flip egg over (*see process illustration*). Cook for another minute to finish. Place finely chopped shrimp in pan, add sugar, salt, and red food coloring (enough to make shrimps pink), and cook for 7–8 minutes mixing well. Place cooked egg on damp cloth, put shrimp mixture in center and *chirashi-zushi* on top. Use cloth to fold egg over shrimp mixture into shape and mold. Turn over and remove cloth to serve. Cut cross on top egg to show pink shrimp mixture.

ちらし壽司

FUKUSA-ZUSHI   CHIRASHI-ZUSHI

47

魚介

**Fish**

SUGATA-MORI

AN EXOTIC WAY to serve your favorite fish and one that will surprise you by its unusual flavor.

Ingredients
    3 1/4 lbs. fresh sea bream
    2 tbsps. flour
    vegetable oil
    1 tbsp. salt
    pon-zu sauce (*see basic recipe page 127*)
    leek for *sarashi-negi* (*see basic recipe page 12*)
    momiji-oroshi (*see basic recipe page 12*)
    2 tbsps. *wari-shio*: mix 3 parts salt with 4 parts cornstarch

Utensils and Equipment
    Skillet; mixing bowls.
Method
    Cut off head of sea bream and remove all flesh from center bone. Cut in fairly large pieces, roll in flour, and deep-fry in 350° oil for 6–7 minutes. Sprinkle 1 tbsp. salt on head and center bone and heat in 450° oven for 15 minutes. Place head and bone on platter and arrange cooked fish as in photograph. Use green pine and folded paper cranes for decoration. Serve with *pon-zu* sauce, *sarashi-negi* and *momiji-oroshi* or with *wari-shio*.
Variations
    Use salmon or sole instead of sea bream.

50

SUGATA-MORI

51

LEMON-YAKI

SALMON SAUTÉED with lemon and served with decorative cucumbers.

Ingredients
   1 lb. salmon cut in 4 slices
   1 tsp. salt
   8 thin slices lemon
   2 cucumbers 8″ long
   2 tbsps. butter
   1/2 tbsp. vegetable oil

Utensils and Equipment
   Skillet with cover.

Method
   Salt salmon and let stand for 10 minutes. Heat butter and oil in skillet, sauté salmon, side with skin down topped by slices of lemon at high heat. Cover, lower heat and cook for 10 minutes. Pare and rub cucumbers with salt. Cut in 2″ lengths, make a 1″ slit in center and cut diagonally to slit from both sides to obtain shape shown in photo. Remove fish to platter, garnish with fresh lemon slices and cucumber.

LEMON-YAKI

KASANE-YAKI

FISH, COMBINED with lemon and tomato slices and sautéed crisply, is as good to eat as it is to look at.

Ingredients
    1 lb. white meat fish fillet cut in 1/4″ slices
    2 medium-sized tomatoes sliced to 1/4″ thickness
    1 lemon sliced thin
    12 small green chili peppers, seeded (substitute bell peppers cut in 12 pieces)
    salt
    pepper
    2 tbsps. vegetable oil

Utensils and Equipment
    Skillet with cover; frying pan.
Method
    Heat 1 tbsp. oil in skillet. Arrange fish, lemon, and tomato in that order, overlapping each other in hot oil, add seasonings. Sauté over medium heat for 1–2 minutes. Cover and cook for 7–8 minutes over low heat. Sauté green pepper separately in 1 tbsp. of oil and sprinkle with salt and pepper. Serve fish, lemon, and tomato on platter, garnished with green pepper.
Variations
    Substitute salmon fillet for white meat fish and onion slices for tomatoes. Make sauce of 1/2 cup tomato catsup and 2 tbsps. Worcestershire and cook 1–2 minutes with fish.

KAORI-YAKI

WHITE MEAT FISH baked with lemon and served with cauliflower and bell pepper.

Ingredients
    1 lb. white meat fish filet, cut in 12 slices
    marinade for fish: 3 tbsps. soy sauce, 2 tbsps. *mirin*, 1 tbsp. *saké*
    1 lemon, sliced thin
    1/2 tbsp. vegetable oil
    1/2 head cauliflower, boiled with dash of vinegar
    1/4 cup *sanbai-zu* (*see basic recipe page 127*) to dip cauliflower
    1 bell pepper, seeded, sliced in thin rings and dipped in boiling water

Utensils and Equipment
    Large bowl to marinate fish; baking pan.
Method
    Marinate fish and let stand for 1 hour. Oil pan and line fish removed from the marinade alternately with lemon slices. Place in medium heat oven and bake for 7–8 minutes. Baste with marinade several times while baking. Dip cauliflower in *sanbai-zu* and serve with fish and bell pepper rings.

香り焼き

KAORI-YAKI

重ね焼き

KASANE-YAKI

55

BUTTER-YAKI

A NOVEL DISH in which clams and *saké* are baked together and then cooked in a special sauce.

Ingredients
　　20 large white clams which have been soaked in salt water 4–5 hours (5 cups of water per 2 tsps. salt)
　　2 tbsps. *saké*
　　3 tbsps. butter
　　sauce: 1/2 cup soy sauce, 3 tbsps. sugar, 2 tbsps. *saké*
　　1 lemon, sliced thin

Utensils and Equipment
　　Covered pan; skillet; saucepan.
Method
　　Bake clams with *saké* in covered pan for about 5 minutes over medium heat. Remove and shell, keeping shells. Sauté clams in butter. In another pan boil soy sauce, sugar, and *saké* until reduced by 1/4. Add clams and cook over high heat for 3–4 minutes, mixing well to obtain maximum flavor and color. Wash shells. Place clams in them and serve with lemon slices. Put a layer of coarse salt on plate and arrange clams with pine needles.
Variations
　　Use oysters instead of clams.

BUTTER-YAKI

KUSHI-YAKI

A NOVEL way to serve tuna—on skewers with green peppers.

Ingredients
1 lb. fresh tuna, sliced in 16 pieces
marinade: 1/3 cup soy sauce, 1 1/2 tbsps. *mirin*, 1 tbsp. sugar
16 small green chili peppers seeded (substitute strips of bell pepper)
2 tbsps. vegetable oil

Utensils and Equipment
16 bamboo skewers; bowl for marinade; skillet with cover of smaller size.

Method
Marinate tuna for about 10 minutes. Put skewers through tuna and green pepper alternately. Heat oil and sauté tuna on both sides over medium heat until slightly brown. Add marinade, lower heat, and cover skillet. Cook for a few minutes, remove cover, and cook at medium heat, shaking pan for another 2–3 minutes. Sprinkle with *shichimi togarashi* or *sansho* just before removing from fire.

TERIYAKI

TUNA, in another completely new style.

Ingredients
1 lb. fresh tuna cut in 4 slices and rolled in flour
1 cucumber 8″ long
1/4 cup *sanbai-zu* (*see basic recipe page 127*)
2 tbsps. vegetable oil
4 tbsps. soy sauce
1 tbsp. *mirin*
2 tbsps. sugar

Utensils and Equipment
Mixing bowl for *sanbai-zu*; skillet with cover of smaller size.

Method
Peel cucumber in spots and cut in 2 inch pieces. Then slice three-quarters way through as thinly as possible, sprinkle with salt, and let stand for 5 minutes. Rinse and marinate in *sanbai-zu*. Heat oil and sauté tuna over medium heat until both sides are slightly brown. Drain oil, add soy sauce, *mirin*, and sugar, cover and cook over low heat until juice is reduced by half. Turn heat up to medium and cook, shaking pan, for 4–5 minutes. Be sure to drain oil before adding soy sauce, *mirin*, and sugar.

串焼き

照り焼き

KUSHI-YAKI

TERIYAKI

59

AEMONO

A TYPICAL *sunomono* served with meat dishes, this has a delicate, fresh flavor.

Ingredients

6–8 oz. scallops boiled, drained, and shredded (canned scallops may be used)

2 cups cucumber, matchstick size, soaked in salt water (solution of 2 tsps. salt in 5 cups water)

1 egg beaten with 1/8 tsp. salt, thinly fried and cut in 1/8″ by 1 1/2″ strips

1 1/2 oz. ginger root, grated and squeezed for juice (use garlic press)

4 tbsps. *sanbai-zu* (*see basic recipe page 127*)

Utensils

Mixing bowl

Method

Put scallops, cucumber, and eggs in *sanbai-zu* and add ginger juice. Mix well and serve.

Variations

Substitute canned shrimps, crab, or boiled fillets of white meat fish.

TEMPURA

THIS UNUSUAL FISH *tempura* is served as a main course
with small green peppers and mushrooms on white grass
paper folded to resemble a crane.

Ingredients
    1 1/2 lbs. white meat fish fillets, cut into 12 slices
    4 dried mushroom caps soaked in water to soften
    8 small green chili peppers, seeded (substitute bell
    peppers cut in 8 pieces)
    1 1/2 cups *tempura* batter: (*see basic recipe page 127*)
    3/4 cup *momiji-oroshi* (*see basic recipe page 12*)
    2 cups *tempura* sauce (*see basic recipe page 127*)
    5 cups deep frying oil (sesame seed oil or vegetable oil)

Utensils
    Mixing bowl; grater; strainer; skillet.
Method
    Wash and dry fish, drain and dry mushrooms. Mix
    tempura batter lightly—do not beat too much. Heat
    oil to 350° (to test, drop a few drops of batter in oil
    —if oil is not hot enough the batter will sink completely,
    if too hot it will sizzle on surface, but if batter stops
    midway, oil is just right). Dip fish in batter and fry
    in oil for 4 minutes. Do the same with mushrooms and
    green peppers. Drain on absorbent paper and serve
    with *tempura* sauce and relish.

62

TEMPURA

天ぷら

SAKA-MUSHI

ABALONE STEAMED in *saké* is a dish that goes well with *saké* and almost anything else.

Ingredients
    2 fresh abalone (9—10 oz.). Clean shells and keep for serving
    3 tbsps. salt to scrub abalone
    2 tsps. salt
    2 tbsps. *saké*
    2 cucumbers 6″ long
    1 oz. pickled red ginger

Utensils and Equipment
    Spatula to remove abalone from shell; steam cooker.
Method
    Cover abalone with salt and scrub well to remove blackish portion. Remove from shell (*see process illustrations*). Scrape off green edges, place abalone in pan, add salt and *saké*, and steam for 20 minutes over high heat. Cool and slice horizontally in two (zigzag) and then cut in 1/2″ pieces. Pare cucumbers, rub well with salt, slice vertically in two and cut in 3/4″ pieces. Cut red ginger in 1/4″ squares. Put abalone and cucumbers in shells and garnish with red ginger. Serve with soy sauce and, if desired, grated horseradish.

64

SAKA-MUSHI

FUNAMORI

BOILED LOBSTER, served in shells, is especially appropriate for festive occasions.

Ingredients
    4 live lobsters (1 1/2 lbs. each)
    1/2 cup soy sauce
    5 tbsps. sugar
    1 cucumber about 6″ long, peeled

Utensils and Equipment
    Pot to boil lobsters; saucepan to cook lobster meat.

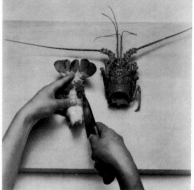

Method
    Place lobsters in pot with cold water barely covering. Bring to a boil and boil briskly for 10 minutes. Take lobsters from pot and let cool. Remove meat from shells as shown in the process photographs and cut meat into 1/2″ pieces. Combine soy sauce and sugar in saucepan and cook for 4-5 minutes after boiling point is reached. Add lobster meat and cook over medium heat for 2-3 minutes, constantly shaking pan. Replace meat in shells to serve. Quarter cucumber vertically and crisp in ice water. Serve as garnish, lightly salted, with lobster. Do not overboil lobsters and be sure to start with cold water.

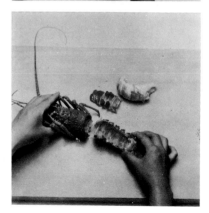

Variations
    Substitute large crabs for lobster.

SUGAKI

OYSTERS MARINATED in grated *daikon* and vinegar are ideal appetizers for *saké* (or whatever) drinkers.

Ingredients
20 medium-sized fresh oysters washed in 1 tsp. salt per 1 cup water solution
2 tsps. vinegar
1/2 cup grated *daikon*
1/4 cup *sanbai-zu* (*see basic recipe page 127*)
pinch finely chopped lemon peel

Utensils and Equipment
Grater; mixing bowl.
Method
Sprinkle oysters with vinegar. Squeeze grated *daikon* lightly, put into sauce and mix. Add oysters and stir together lightly before serving with pinch of chopped lemon peel.
Variations
Add 1 tbsp. *saké* to oysters and vinegar and heat over medium fire before mixing with *daikon* and *sanbai-zu*.

NITSUKE

A NOVEL and simple way to prepare fish for either fish course or first course.

Ingredients
1 lb. white meat fish filet, cut in 8 pieces
7 oz. bamboo shoots (boiled, canned), cut in 1″ pieces
1 cup water
1/2 cup *mirin*
1/3 cup *saké*
2 1/2 tbsps. sugar
4 1/2 tbsps. soy sauce
4 oz. string beans, lightly boiled in salt water
1/2 cup soup stock (*see basic recipe page 127*) combined with 1/2 tsp. each soy sauce, *mirin*, and sugar

Utensils and Equipment
Pan with cover of slightly smaller size; saucepan.
Method
Place fillets in pan with *mirin*, *saké*, and water and cover. Bring to a boil, reduce to medium heat, add sugar and cook for 4-5 minutes. Add half soy sauce and cook for 7-8 minutes. Add remaining soy, bring to a boil, and turn off heat. Remove fish and cook bamboo shoots in same mixture for 2-3 minutes. Heat boiled string beans in soup stock mixture to boiling point, turn off heat and let stand to cool. Serve fish with bamboo shoots and string beans cut in halves. Pour fish-bamboo juice over all.

酢牡蠣

SUGAKI

NITSUKE

煮つけ

SUNOMONO

AN EXCELLENT luncheon dish—fresh crab, boiled and served with cucumbers and a vinegar sauce.

Ingredients
    4 live crabs (approx. 3/4 lb. each)
    dash salt
    3/4 cup *nihai-zu* (*see basic recipe page 127*)
    2 6″ cucumbers cut in 2″ length sticks

Utensils and Equipment
    Mixing bowl; saucepan.
Method
    Barely cover crabs with water and add a dash of salt. Boil for 10 minutes after reaching boiling point. Cool and remove legs and cut aslant to facilitate eating. Remove meat from body and slice horizontally in two. Clean shell and replace meat. Serve cucumbers on side and use vinegar sauce as dip.
Variations
    Substitute boiled shrimp for crab. Serve crab with tartar sauce or mayonnaise sauce.

SUNOMONO

71

鶏肉

Chicken

TATSUTA-AGE

CUT UP CHICKEN, marinated in a typical Japanese manner and then deep fried, makes an unusual main course.

Ingredients
    1 1/2 lbs. chicken, cut in approximately 1 1/2″ pieces
    marinade: 4 tbsps. soy, 1 tbsp. sugar, 2 tbsps. *saké*
    3 tbsps. cornstarch
    5 cups vegetable oil
    sansho or mustard

Utensils and Equipment
    Large bowl to marinate chicken; skillet.
Method
    Marinate chicken for about 30 minutes. Remove and roll in cornstarch and let stand for 10 minutes. Fry in 350° oil over medium heat until crisp and brown (about 3 minutes). Serve with *sansho* or mustard.
Variations
    Use fillet of fish instead of chicken. Serve with *sunomono* and *miso* soup.

74

龍田揚げ

TATSUTA-AGE

TERIYAKI

ALTHOUGH MOST Westerners are familiar with *teriyaki* in various forms, this chicken *teriyaki* has a surprisingly different taste.

Ingredients
    1 lb. chicken breasts
    marinade: 2 tbsps. sugar, 2 tbsps. *mirin*, 5 tbsps. soy
    4 tbsps. vegetable oil
    12 small green chili peppers
    dash salt
    dash pepper

Utensils and Equipment
    Mixing bowl; skillet with cover; frying pan.
Method
    Pierce skin of chicken with fork (*see process illustration*), and dip in boiling water for about 10 seconds. Heat 3 tbsps. oil and sauté chicken over high heat until browned. Drain off oil, pour in marinade, and cook covered for 7–8 minutes over low heat. Remove cover and cook, shaking skillet over medium heat until marinade is almost cooked away. Cool and slice in 1/4″ pieces to serve. Sauté peppers until crisp, sprinkle with salt and pepper, serve as garnish on chicken. Be sure to drain oil before pouring marinade in frying pan.
Variations
    Use duck, wild if possible, or pork instead of chicken. Stick green peppers on skewers and deep fry to serve.

76

TERIYAKI

照り焼き

IRI-DORI

A WHOLE MEAL in one dish, this unusual sautéed chicken makes a delicious casserole for bridge luncheons or buffet suppers.

Ingredients
   12 oz. chicken breast cut into 1/2″ squares
   1 carrot, diced
   4 dried mushroom caps softened in water and quartered
   7 oz. boiled bamboo shoots, diced
   1 1/2 tbsps. vegetable oil
   4 tbsps. soup stock (*see basic recipe page 127*)
   4 tbsps. *mirin*
   4 tbsps. sugar
   4 tbsps. soy sauce
   3 tbsps. canned green peas (or fresh or frozen, lightly boiled)

Utensils and Equipment
   Skillet.

Method
   Heat oil in pan and sauté chicken, carrots, mushrooms, and bamboo shoots over high heat for 1–2 minutes. Add soup stock, *mirin*, sugar and cook for 10 minutes. Turn heat to medium, add soy sauce, and cook until sauce is reduced to about 1/4. Add peas just before removing from heat.

Variations
   Use deep-fried fish instead of chicken, or add any of the following: cauliflower, brussel sprouts, onion, celery.

IRI-DORI

79

SAKA-MUSHI

TENDER BONED chicken breasts, steamed with saké, are served sliced and cold with a tangy horseradish dip.

Ingredients
  1 lb. chicken breasts
  2 tsps. salt
  2 tbsps. *saké*
  2 cucumbers 8″ long
  1 *wasabi* grated or 2 tsps. powdered horseradish mixed into paste with water
  4 lettuce leaves

Utensils and Equipment
  Grater; steam cooker; chopping block.

Method
  Pierce skin of chicken (*see illustration page 76*). Salt lightly and pour *saké* over chicken and rub in well. Steam for 15 minutes over high heat, remove and cool. Rub cucumber well with salt, cut in inch-long pieces and then slice to 1/8″ thickness. Grate *wasabi* and pound on chopping block to form paste. Slice chicken to 3/4″ thickness and serve with cucumbers on lettuce. Mix *wasabi* with soy sauce for dip.

Variations
  Use duck, wild if possible, instead of chicken, but in this case dip in boiling water to remove odor. Use mayonnaise in place of horseradish dip.

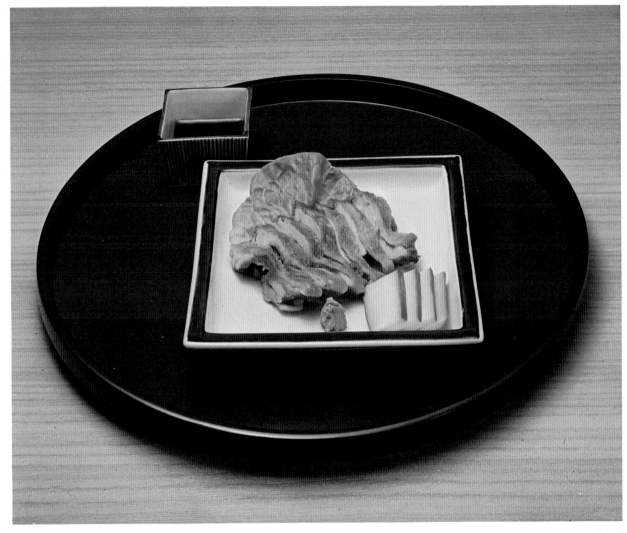

SAKA-MUSHI

TORI-SUKI

THE POPULAR international favorite—*sukiyaki*—is given here in a brand new version which uses chicken in place of beef.

Ingredients

    3 lbs. chicken boned and cut in small pieces
    soup stock: 5 cups water, 1 cup soy sauce, 1/3 cup *mirin* or 4 tbsps. sugar, chicken bones, and giblets
    6 oz. *shirataki*, lightly boiled and cut in 2″ lengths
    2 carrots sliced and lightly boiled
    2 leeks cut in 1 1/2″ lengths

Utensils and Equipment

    Heavy pan or skillet; *hibachi*, or brazier. This dish may be started in the kitchen and then cooked on a *hibachi* at the table.

Method

    Put chicken bones and giblets in water, add soy sauce, *mirin* or sugar, and simmer for 40–50 minutes. Remove bones (*see process illustration*), and add chicken. Remove skillet to *hibachi* and continue cooking until chicken is almost done. Add *shirataki* and vegetables. Serve and eat while cooking. To avoid overcooking, add ingredients gradually, a bit at a time, and serve when done.

Variations

    Use beef or pork or add clams to chicken. Use other vegetables such as spinach or mushrooms.

TORISUKI

牛肉

Beef

KUZU-TATAKI

AN EXOTIC BEEF dish that can be prepared well in advance and served with pride as an entree on a hot summer evening.

Ingredients
    1 lb. beef (tenderloin, sirloin, or rib roast) 1/4″ thick, cut in 1 1/2″ by 1/2″ slices
    1/2 stalk celery, cleaned and sliced in 1 1/2″ strips
    4 bell peppers, seeds removed and quartered
    2/3 cup cornstarch, sifted
    salt
    1/2 cup *momiji-oroshi* (*see basic recipe page 12*)
    sarashi-negi (*see basic recipe page 12*)
    3/4 cup *pon-zu* sauce (*see basic recipe page 127*)

Utensils and Equipment
    Strainer; ice water; large kettle; colander.

Method
Fill large kettle 3/4 full with water (add 1 tbsp. salt for every 5 cups of water); bring water to boil. Roll meat, celery, and bell pepper in cornstarch. Have pan of ice water at hand. Drop celery in boiling water and remove when water boils again. Place immediately in ice water to chill suddenly. Remove and drain in colander. Do same to bell peppers. Repeat process with beef, doing about 1/3 of quantity at a time. Place meat and vegetables in refrigerator until serving time. Put 1 tbsp. each of *momiji-oroshi* and *sarashi-negi* in *pon-zu* sauce and use as a dip. Do not overboil vegetables or beef.

Variations
Use vinegar instead of *pon-zu*. Substitute white meat fish fillet or chicken for beef.

86

葛たたき

KUZU-TATAKI

87

KUSHI-YAKI

THIS DELIGHTFUL beef and onion on skewers can be the main course at your next barbecue. It's different!

Ingredients
1 lb. beef, cut in 1 1/4″ × 3/4″ × 3/4″ strips
4 leeks—use white part only and cut in 1 1/4″ lengths
2 tbsps. flour
2 tbsps. vegetable oil
1/2 cup soy sauce
4 tbsps. sugar
2 tbsps. *mirin*
1/2 lemon cut in 8 slices
sansho or finely ground pepper

Utensils and Equipment
8 bamboo skewers; skillet with cover

Method
String beef and leeks alternately on bamboo skewers, then roll in flour. Heat oil in skillet and sear meat over medium heat until both sides are brown. Drain off oil and add soy sauce, sugar, *mirin*. Cover and cook each side for 2–3 minutes. Remove and simmer juice until it is reduced to about half of the original quantity. Return skewers to skillet to heighten color. Serve with lemon and *sansho* while hot.

Variations
Substitute pork, chicken, liver for beef and white onion for leek. Barbecue on grill. In this case, use skillet to brown both sides of meat and then place on grill and cook while basting with soy sauce, sugar, *mirin* mixture.

TSUKE-YAKI

FOR GOURMENTS here is beef steak marinated in soy sauce and *sansho* or ginger to give that authentic Oriental flavor. For extra flourish, serve with sautéed eggplant.

Ingredients
4 steaks
marinade per pound of meat: 5 tbsps. soy sauce, 3 tbsps. *mirin*, dash *sansho* or grated ginger root juice (use garlic press)
3 tbsps. vegetable oil
1 medium-sized eggplant. Remove top, score, cut in 2″ pieces
dash salt
mustard

Utensils and Equipment
Mixing bowl; 2 skillets.
Method
Marinate steaks for 45–50 minutes. Heat 1 tbsp. oil in skillet and sear steaks until both sides are brown. Pour marinade in pan and cook 3–5 minutes, turning steaks to heighten color. Sauté eggplant in 2 tbsps. oil for 3 minutes. Sprinkle with salt and serve with steaks. Mustard on the side for those who want it.
Variations
Use pork instead of beef.

つけ焼

TSUKE-YAKI

91

TOBAN-YAKI

GRILLED BEEF, marinated first, then served with green peppers and sesame salt.

Ingredients
   1 1/2 lbs. tenderloin, sliced 1/2" thick
   4 bell peppers, seeded and cut vertically in halves
   marinade: 1/3 cup soy sauce, 4 tbsps. sugar, 1 tbsp.
   mirin, 1 leek chopped fine (or small clove of garlic)
   oil for griddle
   goma-shio (see basic recipe page 14)
   sauce: mixture of 1:1/3 of catsup and Worcestershire sauce

Utensils and Equipment
   Mixing bowl; griddle or heavy skillet.
Method
   Soak beef in marinade for about 15 minutes. Oil griddle
   and grill beef and bell peppers to desired doneness.
   Serve in casserole with sesame salt or sauce.
Variations
   Substitute pork, chicken, or shrimp. Meat may be
   barbecued. Fresh mushrooms, tomatoes, or eggplant
   may also be used.

TOBAN-YAKI

93

GINGAMI-YAKI

STRIPS OF TENDER beef roasted in foil with fresh vegetables. Good for indoor or outdoor dining.

Ingredients
1 lb. beef (tenderloin, sirloin or rib roast) sliced 1/8″ thick, cut in 1 1/2″ strips
2 bell peppers, seeds removed and cut in 3 or 4 pieces
1 stalk celery, cleaned and cut in 1″ lengths
8 dried mushroom caps, softened in water and cut in halves
3 tbsps. butter
1 tsp. salt
1/2 tsp. pepper
1/2 cup *pon-zu* sauce (*see basic recipe page 127*)
1/2 cup *momiji-oroshi* (*see basic recipe page 12*)
1 leek for *sarashi-negi* (*see basic recipe page 12*)

Utensils and Equipment
4 ten-inch squares of foil.

Method
Salt and pepper meat, butter center of the foil, place meat, mushrooms, pepper, and celery on top in this order and sprinkle with salt. Wrap securely and put in oven at high temperature for 15 minutes. Serve while hot with *momiji-oroshi* and *sarashi-negi* in *pon-zu* sauce.

Variations
Use chicken, shrimp, or white meat fish instead of beef. Use fresh mushrooms if available.

GINGAMI-YAKI

95

豚肉

Pork

TERIYAKI

A VERY FANCY but simple to prepare pork and onion combination that is excellent with cocktails, *saké*, or beer.

Ingredients

8 bacon-thin slices of pork
8 leeks, use white tips only
1/4 cup *saké*
3 tbsps. sugar
1/3 cup soy sauce
2 tbsps. oil
2 cucumbers cut in 2″ lengths. Peel skin to form square and cut vertically in fours.
dash vinegar
dash salt

Utensils and Equipment

8 toothpicks; skillet with cover.

Method

Wrap pork firmly around white part of leek (*see process illustration*) and secure with toothpick. Prepare mixture of soy sauce, sugar, and *saké*. Heat oil and cook pork over medium heat until brown on all sides. Drain oil, lower heat, pour in soy mixture. Cover and cook for 2–3 minutes turning constantly to cook all sides. Remove cover, turn heat to medium again, and cook, shaking pan to heighten color. Remove from skillet, take out toothpicks. Cut in 1″ lengths to serve. Salt cucumbers lightly and sprinkle with vinegar. Serve as garnish with pork.

Variations

Substitute thin slices of white meat chicken or strips of white meat fish fillet. Use mushrooms or boiled string beans for center instead of leek.

98

TERIYAKI

AMI-YAKI

THIS DIFFERENT barbecued pork dish is simple to prepare and has a zesty flavor that will bring requests for second helpings.

Ingredients

    1-1 1/2 lbs. pork tenderloin, cut in 1/4″ slices
    dash salt
    3 oz. pickled red ginger sliced thinly
    soy sauce dip: 2 tsps. ginger root juice, 1 clove finely chopped garlic, 2 tsps. onion juice, 1/2 cup soy sauce, 2 tbsps. *saké*, 1 tbsp. sugar, 2 tbsps. vegetable oil. Mix well together.

Utensils and Equipment

    Grater or garlic press; mixing bowl; meat pounder; grill, *hibachi* or brazier.

Method

    Pound tenderloin lightly and sprinkle with salt. Prepare soy sauce dip. Cook meat on grill until tender. Dip in sauce and serve hot.

Variations

    Marinate pork in soy sauce mixture for 2–3 minutes before cooking. Use skillet instead of grill. Substitute beef or lamb for pork. Serve with mustard or *sansho*.

AMI-YAKI

NIKOMI

SPARERIBS GET a novel treatment in this taste-tempting meal-in-one-dish which is especially good in cold weather.

Ingredients
>1 lb. pork spareribs, cut in 1/2″ pieces
>4 medium-sized potatoes, whole, peeled
>1 2″ *daikon*, sliced in 8 pieces
>2 large carrots, cut in large cubes, edges rounded
>1 handful string beans
>2 tbsps. vegetable oil
>4 tbsps. sugar
>2 tbsps. *saké*
>1/3 cup soy sauce

Utensils and Equipment
>Skillet with cover; saucepan.

Method
>Heat oil in skillet and cook pork over strong heat for 1–2 minutes. Then add potatoes, *daikon*, and carrots and cook for another 1–2 minutes. Lower heat to medium, add water to barely cover contents, sugar, and *saké*. Cover and cook for 7–8 minutes. Then turn heat to low, add soy sauce and cook for another 14–15 minutes. Boil string beans for 3–4 minutes, cut in 1″ lengths, and add to other ingredients. Be sure to turn heat low after adding soy sauce.

Variations
>Use chicken or shrimp instead of pork. Use sherry or white wine instead of *saké*.

NIKOMI

AGE-BUTA

AN UNUSUAL method of cooking pork that brings out its delicate flavor. Serve hot or cold.

Ingredients
    1 lb. pork, cut in 1 1/2-2″ square strips along the grain
    5 cups vegetable oil
    1 large tomato
    2 tbsps. soy sauce
    1/2 tsp. pepper
    mustard

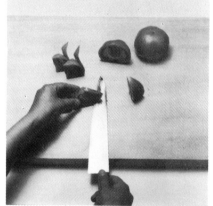

Utensils and Equipment
    Deep fryer.

Method
    Heat oil to 350° and deep fry pork over medium to low heat for 4–5 minutes, or until tender. Remove and sprinkle well with soy sauce and pepper. Cut into 1/4″ thick slices and serve with mustard. Slice tomato in 8 pieces, peeling skin back part way and garnish platter (*see process illustration*).

Variations
    Shred pork and mix with boiled bean sprouts or sliced cucumbers in vinegar sauce (1 cup vinegar, 3 tbsps. sugar, and 1 tsp. salt) to make *sunomono*.

揚げ豚

AGE-BUTA

105

KAKUNI

A HEARTY PORK and vegetable casserole using spareribs sparked with ginger, *saké*, and soy. Potatoes are the perfect accompaniment.

Ingredients
1 lb. pork spareribs diced in 1″ squares
1 oz. ginger root, sliced thin
2 tbsps. vegetable oil
3 tbsps. *saké*
4 tbsps. soy sauce
2 tbsps. sugar
1 handful string beans
pinch salt

Utensils and Equipment
Skillet with cover; saucepan.
Method
Heat oil over medium heat. Sauté sliced ginger briefly, then add pork and cook to brown all sides. Lower heat, add water to barely cover, and *saké*. Cover and cook for 1 hour. When pork is tender add soy sauce, and sugar, and cook until juice is almost completely absorbed. Cook string beans lightly, cut in 1″ lengths and serve with pork.
Variations
Sprinkle with grated lemon peel to serve.

角煮

ひき肉

Ground Meat

OBORO

Hot RICE with ground chicken, eggs, and vegetables makes a tempting brunch or luncheon dish.

Ingredients
    10 oz. ground chicken meat
    1 1/2 tbsps. vegetable oil
    2 tbsps. sugar
    2 tbsps. *mirin*
    5 tbsps. soy sauce
    4 large dried mushroom caps, softened in water (keep water)
    1 tbsp. sugar
    2 tbsps. *mirin*
    1 tbsp. soy sauce
    2 eggs, lightly beaten with dash of salt
    1 oz. string beans, with water to barely cover
    2 radishes
    4 cups cooked rice (*see basic recipe page 127*)

Utensils and Equipment
    2 skillets; 2 saucepans; egg beater.

Method
Sauté chicken in vegetable oil over medium heat, mixing well. Add sugar, *mirin*, and soy sauce and cook over low heat until liquids are thoroughly blended, about 7–8 minutes. Remove from heat but keep warm. Cook mushrooms barely covered by the water in which they were soaked for 4–5 minutes, then add sugar, *mirin*, and soy sauce. Continue cooking over low heat until water boils away. Pour egg mixture into lightly greased skillet and fry over medium heat to thin pancake consistency. Cool and cut in strips 1 1/2″ by 1/2″. Boil string beans lightly, remove, drain, and slice in thin strips. Slice radishes thin and chill in ice water. Place hot rice in a serving bowl, cover with ground chicken, mushrooms which have been slivered, and top with egg, string beans, and radish slices. Rice and chicken should be hot to absorb vegetable and egg flavors.

OBORO

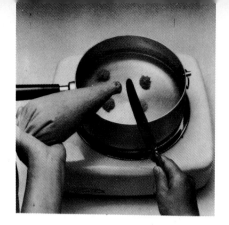

SUMASHI-JIRU

THIS CLEAR SOUP with meat balls, noodles, and *mitsuba*, is delicious and unusual.

Ingredients

    1/2 lb. twice ground meat (half beef and half pork)
    1 oz. grated ginger root juice (use garlic press)
    2/3 tbsps. flour
    2 eggs
    5 cups water
    4 small carrots, cut in cubes, edges rounded and slightly boiled
    1 oz. boiled noodles (the thinner the better)
    4 strands *mitsuba*, cut in 1″ pieces
    2/3 tsp. salt
    1 tsp. soy sauce

Utensils and Equipment

    Mixing bowl; pastry bag; soup pot.

Method

Mix ground meat, ginger juice, flour, and eggs well and stuff into pastry bag. Bring to a boil 5 cups of water and add carrots. Then drop meat mixture by squeezing from pastry bag and cutting off meat balls into water and carrots. Cook over low heat for 10 minutes, skimming off foam and floating fat. Add seasonings and drop in noodles and *mitsuba* just before turning off heat. To obtain a clear soup, be careful not to overcook.

Variations

Use salmon, white meat fish, or shrimp balls instead of beef-pork. Meat balls can be formed with a tablespoon instead of pastry bag.

SUMASHI-JIRU

SUEHIRO-YAKI

FAN-SHAPED ground chicken patties, these delicacies make tempting hors d'oeuvres.

Ingredients
    10 oz. chicken meat
    2 eggs
    2 1/2 tbsps. flour
    1 1/2 tbsps. sugar
    2/3 tsp. salt
    1 1/2 tbsps. soy sauce
    1 1/2 tbsps. *mirin*, or 1 1/2 tbsps. *saké* and 1 1/2 tbsps. sugar
    2 tbsps. vegetable oil
    1 sheet *nori*, dried and crushed
    1 tsp. poppy seeds
    2 oz. pickled red ginger, diced

Utensils and Equipment
    Earthenware mortar (or food grinder); skillet.
Method
    Grind chicken meat well, add eggs and flour, and mix together. Add sugar, salt, soy sauce, and *mirin*, combining thoroughly to form paste. Divide mixture into two equal parts for ease in cooking. Spread a 1/2" thick layer in the skillet in which 1 tbsp. of oil has been heated. Sprinkle with *aonori* and poppy seeds. Sauté over light heat until both sides are browned evenly. Remove from pan and repeat cooking process with other half of mixture. Cut into fan-shaped pieces and serve on toothpicks with pickled ginger.

114

HAKATA-MUSHI

GOOD AS an appetizer or first course.

Ingredients
    1 lb. ground meat (half beef and half pork)
    2 tbsps. flour
    1 1/2 tsps. salt
    1 tbsp. soy sauce
    3 eggs, beaten
    1 lb. cabbage, boiled and salted
    special sauce ingredients: 2 cups soup stock (*see basic recipe page 127*), 2/3 tsp. salt
    2 tsps. soy sauce, 1 tbsp. cornstarch

Utensils and Equipment
    Mixing bowl; 6 inch mold; steam cooker; saucepan.
Method
    Mix together well meat, flour, salt, soy sauce, and 1/3 of beaten eggs. Line bottom of mold with 1/3 of cabbage leaves and pour 1/2 of beaten eggs over them. Cover with 1/2" layer of meat mixture, followed by another 1/3 of cabbage leaves and 1/2" layer of meat. Pour remainder of eggs evenly over meat layer and cover with rest of the cabbage leaves. Press lightly and cover with silver foil. Place mold in vigorously boiling steamer and cook for 15 minutes. Prepare sauce by bringing soup stock to a boil. Add salt and soy sauce and when boiling point is reached, thicken with cornstarch. Mix slowly for a few minutes. Cool meat-cabbage mixture and cut in 1 1/2" squares. Serve with sauce.

末廣焼き

SUEHIRO-YAKI

博多蒸し

HAKATA-MUSHI

115

KUSHI-DANGO

FRENCH-FRIED meat balls, served on bright green bamboo skewers, are a new taste treat. The decorative "flowers" are typical of Japanese cookery.

Ingredients
    12 oz. ground meat (half beef, half pork)
    2 tsps. grated cheese
    2 stalks celery, chopped fine
    2 eggs
    3 tbsps. flour
    1 tsp. salt
    dash pepper
    5 cups vegetable oil
    1 *daikon*, peeled and cut in 1″ pieces
    marinade for *daikon:* 4 tbsps. *sanbai-zu* (*see basic recipe page 127*)
    1 hard-boiled egg yolk, chopped fine
    celery leaves

Utensils and Equipment
    Mixing bowl; skillet; 12 bamboo skewers (or large toothpicks).

Method
    Mix ground meat with cheese, celery, eggs, and flour until sticky. Season with salt and pepper. Form into 1″ diameter balls and deep fry at 350° until brown. Put three balls on each skewer. Slice *daikon* in fine strips, leaving 1/4″ base uncut; cut in 1″ squares, sprinkle with salt, and marinate for 1–2 hours. Arrange *daikon* to resemble chrysanthemums, placing egg yolk in center and celery leaves on sides for a flower-like effect.

Variations
    Use fish balls instead of meat. Serve balls on toothpicks stuck in cabbage head or pumpkin. Serve with pickled beets or other pickled vegetables.

KUSHI-DANGO

117

デザート

Desserts

KURI-KINTON

A FAVORITE SWEET dessert which is a must on New Year's Day menus in Japan and would be good on all special holidays in the U.S.A.

Ingredients
    10 oz. sweet potatoes, peeled and soaked in water overnight
    1 1/4 cups sugar
    12 canned sweet chestnuts, cut in halves
    1/2 cup syrup (from canned chestnuts)
    1/2 cup water
    1 tbsp. cornstarch

Utensils and Equipment
    3 saucepans; sieve; wet cloth.
Method
    Boil sweet potatoes, mash, and press through sieve. Cook potato with sugar for 12 minutes over very low heat mixing well and then cool. Place two chestnut halves on wet cloth, cover with cooked potato, use cloth to wrap and mold into balls. Cook syrup with 1/2 cup water and cornstarch over low heat mixing well for 2–3 minutes. Pour syrup over chestnut-sweet potato ball and serve.
Variations
    Substitute walnuts for chestnuts. In this case, peel thin walnut skin by dipping in luke warm water.

KOGANE-YAKI

A SWEET that is really different— delicious, pretty to look at, and served on skewers!

Ingredients
    1 loaf *kanten*, soaked in water for 1 hour (or 3 envelopes unflavored gelatin, softened in 1/2 cup water)
    1 1/2 cups water
    1 1/2 cups sugar
    2 eggs, separated
    3 tbsps. sugar
    sprigs of flat, piquant leaves
    1 tsp. cornstarch
    vegetable oil

Utensils and Equipment
    Pan; mixing bowl; mold 6″ × 8″ × 1″; skillet; 24 skewers.
Method
    Cook *kanten* in water over low heat and mix until dissolved. Add sugar and cook for 7–8 minutes until thick. Place pan in water to cool. Beat egg whites until stiff, add sugar and mix well. Pour *kanten* mixture slowly in egg whites, mix well, and pour into mold to set and chill, about 20 minutes. Remove from mold and cut in 1″ by 2″ squares, roll in cornstarch, dip in egg yolk, affix leaf design and cook in skillet over low heat for 30–40 seconds. Place on bamboo skewers to serve.

KORI-SUIKA KURI-KINTON
KOGANE-YAKI AWAYUKI-KAN

AWAYUKI-KAN

A FESTIVE DESSERT that is light and delicate, and a happy ending for a hearty meal. Japanese strawberries are noted for their enormous size and unbelievable flavor.

Ingredients
    10 oz. fresh strawberries, rinsed in salt water
    1 cup water
    1 1/4 cup sugar
    3 envelopes unflavored gelatin, slftened in 1/2 cup water
    2 egg whites
    3 tbsps. sugar
    Custard sauce: 2 egg yolks, 1 tbsp. flour, 1 cup milk, 4 1/2 tbsps. sugar, dash vanilla

Utensils and Equipment
    Circular mold; mixing bowl; egg beater, saucepans.
Method
    Stem half the strawberries and line neatly in mold. Put water and sugar in pan and boil. Add softened gelatin, combining thoroughly. Beat egg whites stiff, add sugar and mix well. Place gelatin pan in cold water and pour in egg whites gradually, while mixing and then beat well. Pour mixture slowly into mold and chill 15-20 minutes until set. Custard sauce: Mix egg yolk, flour, sugar well in pan and pour in warm milk while mixing over low heat. Remove from fire, add vanilla, and chill. Unmold strawberry-egg white mixture on plate, fill center with remainder of strawberries. Serve with chilled custard sauce.

KORI-SUIKA

WATERMELON in a basket! A new way to serve an old favorite hot weather dessert.

Ingredients
    1 watermelon (about 4 1/2 lbs.)
    1 1/2 cups water
    2 cups sugar
    1/2 lemon sliced thin
    Ice cubes

Utensils and Equipment
    Knife; saucepan; spoon or ball cutter.
Method
    Cut watermelon in shape of basket, remove meat using spoon or ball cutter. Boil sugar and water to make sugar syrup and cool. Place ice cubes and melon balls in basket, pour syrup over watermelon, and decorate with lemon slices.

NAMBAN-ZUKE

FOR A NEW TASTE, try marinated deep-fried salmon garnished with crisp onion slices and green pepper. (serves six)

Ingredients

    8 oz. salmon, sliced into 6 pieces, salted and rolled in flour
    1 small onion sliced into rings and crisped in ice water
    1/2 bell pepper, dipped in hot water, cleaned, and cut into thin slices
    marinade for salmon: 2 tbsps. vinegar, 6 tbsps. vegetable oil, 2 tsps. minced parsley
    vegetable oil for deep frying

Utensils and Equipment

    Mixing bowl; skillet.

Method

    Heat oil and deep fry salmon at 350° for 3 minutes. Remove and place in marinade. Fry onion and bell pepper until crisp, and serve as garnish for salmon.

Variations

    Substitute any firm white meat fish. Serve with raw radish slices.

TSUKE-YAKI

SAUTÉED CLAMS with an Oriental twist. (serves six)

Ingredients

    6 large clams boiled and shelled. Keep shells for serving.
    marinade: 3 tbsps. *mirin*, 3 tbsps. soy sauce
    2 tbsps. flour
    1 tbsp. vegetable oil
    dash pepper

Utensils and Equipment

    Mixing bowl: skillet.

Method

    Marinate clams for a few minutes, then roll in flour. Sauté clams briskly over high heat until evenly brown. Lower heat and pour marinade in pan to flavor. Simmer for 20 minutes. Pepper just before removing from pan. Serve in shells and use squares of golden paper for decoration.

MEIGETSU-TAMAGO

A variation of our popular deviled eggs. (serves six)

Ingredients

    3 hard-boiled eggs
    2 tsps. mayonnaise

Method

    Cut eggs in half. Mix yolk with mayonnaise and sieve. Cut ends of eggs slightly for balance and refill yolk.

Variations

    Use peanut butter, grated cheese, or tomato catsup instead of mayonnaise.

TOFU-DENGAKU

TOFU WITH MISO paste makes an unusual appetizer to serve with cocktails. (serves six)

Ingredients

    5 oz. *tofu*, well drained sliced in 2″ by 3/4″ pieces
    1 oz. *miso*
    2 tbsps. *mirin*
    2 tbsps. soup stock (*see basic recipe page 127*)
    2 strands spinach, boiled and puréed through a sieve

Utensils and Equipment

    Steam cooker; sieve; saucepan; 6 bamboo skewers.

Method

    Steam *tofu* in covered pan over strong heat for 5–6 minutes. Combine *miso*, *mirin*, and soup stock over low heat until a paste is formed. Add puréed spinach. Serve *tofu* on skewers well coated with generous serving of this paste.

Variations

    Tofu may be baked with *miso* paste in a high temperature oven for 2–3 minutes.

Origami

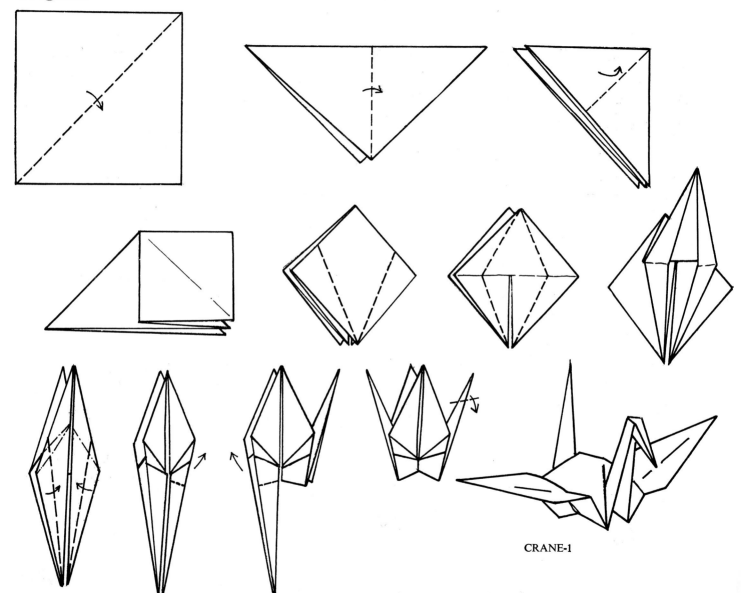

CRANE-1

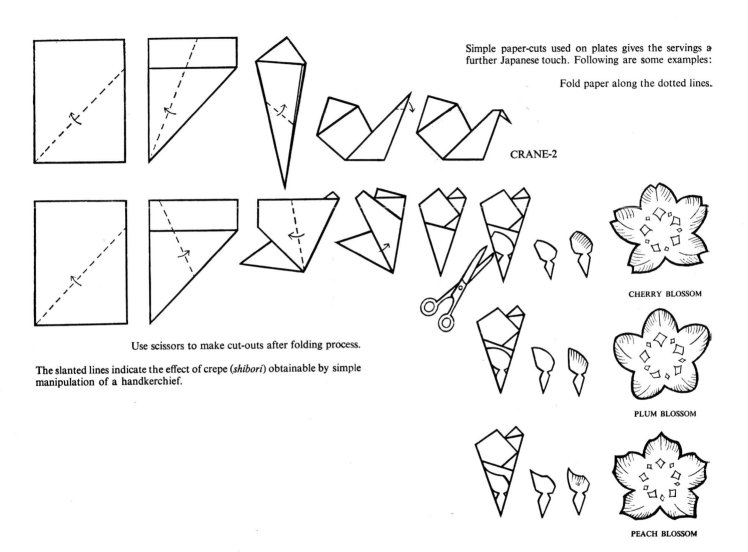

Simple paper-cuts used on plates gives the servings a further Japanese touch. Following are some examples:

Fold paper along the dotted lines.

CRANE-2

CHERRY BLOSSOM

PLUM BLOSSOM

PEACH BLOSSOM

Use scissors to make cut-outs after folding process.

The slanted lines indicate the effect of crepe (*shibori*) obtainable by simple manipulation of a handkerchief.

125

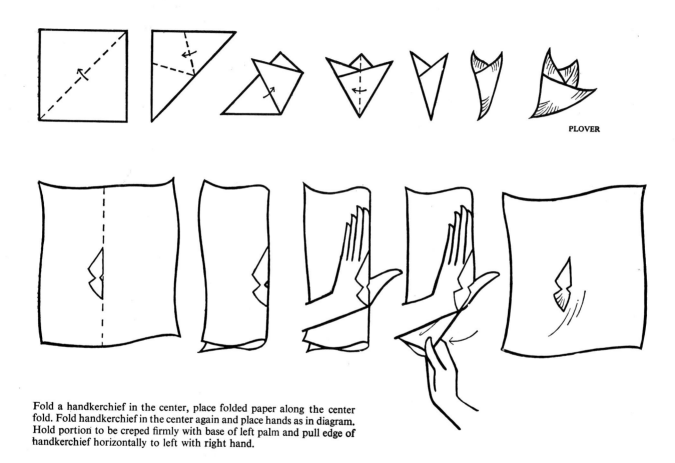

PLOVER

Fold a handkerchief in the center, place folded paper along the center fold. Fold handkerchief in the center again and place hands as in diagram. Hold portion to be creped firmly with base of left palm and pull edge of handkerchief horizontally to left with right hand.

Basic Recipes

Nihai-zu: Vinegar marinade for boiled crab, lobster, shrimp, etc. Mix 1/2 cup vinegar, 1/4 cup soy sauce, 1 tbsp. sugar.

Pon-zu Sauce: Dip for *mizutaki*. Mix 1/2 cup sour orange juice or lemon juice, 1/2 cup soy sauce, 1/2 cup soup stock.

Rice: Wash rice well. Rice and water ratio 1: 1.2 respectively. Cook in thick pan with heavy cover over strong heat until it boils and then turn heat low for 15 minutes. Let stand for another 15 minutes after turning heat off. Slightly decrease water (1: 1.1) when cooking rice for *sushi*.

Sanbai-zu: Vinegar marinade for *sunomono*, etc. Mix 1/2 cup vinegar, 2 tbsps. sugar, 1/2 tsp. soy sauce, 1/2 tsp. salt.

Soup stock: 5 cups water, 1 piece 1 1/2″ square *dashi konbu*, 1/4 to 1/2 oz. shaved *katsuo-bushi*. Method: Wipe *konbu* with wet cloth, place in pan and boil. Remove *konbu* just before boiling point, turn heat to medium and put *katsuo-bushi* shavings in. Turn heat off just before boiling point, leave until shavings settle and then strain. First strain is used for clear soups. For *miso* soups and ordinary cooking, continue to boil *katsuo-bushi* until water is reduced by 1/5. Strain to use.

Tempura Batter: 1/2 beaten egg, 4/5 cup cold water, 1 cup flour. Method: Sift flour and mix with water and beaten egg. Use thick chopsticks and mix lightly. Increase water to 1 cup and use 1 whole egg for fish or clam *tempura*. Decrease water slightly for vegetable *tempura*. Use cold water.

Tempura Sauce: 1 cup water, 1/2 cup each soy sauce, *mirin*, *katsuo-bushi* shavings. Method: Bring ingredients to boiling point, and then strain. Cool to use as dip for *tempura*.

Warishita: Mixture of soy sauce, soup stock, *mirin* (sugar and *saké*), etc. used to cook *sukiyaki*. The ratio of contents varies by the ingredients to be cooked and personal taste. *Tori-suki:* Equal amounts of soy sauce, *mirin*, soup stock (add sugar if preferred sweet) (substitute for *mirin*: *saké* and sugar at the ratio of 1: 1 1/2 respectively). Beef *sukiyaki*: Mixture of soy sauce, *mirin* and sugar at the ratio of 2: 1: 1 respectively. Adjust according to taste by adding sugar or *mirin*. (substitute *saké* for *mirin* and add 1/2 the quantity of sugar.)

Glossary

abrura-age: Fried, thin slices of *tofu*.

daikon: Giant white radish. Turnips can be substituted.

dashi-konbu: Dried kelp used as a soup stock base.

fu: A light "crouton" made of wheat gluten; used in *sukiyaki*, soups, and one-pot cookery.

ginger root: Fresh ginger is costly and is usually available in the West, depending on the locality. If at all possible, however, fresh ginger should be used in preference to powdered; the succulence and delicate flavor make a world of difference.

ginger, pickled red: An excellent garnish also for many occasions other than a Japanese repast.

goma: Sesame seeds. There are two varieties, white and black.

goma-shio: Sesame seeds mixed with table salt. This should be available in convenient shakers, but can be easily made at home. (recipe p. 14).

green chili peppers: The small green chili used in Japanese cooking is sweet and not hot. Bell pepper is an adequate substitute.

hakusai: Chinese cabbage. Round cabbage can be substituted, if necessary.

kanten: Agar-agar; used as a gelatin. Health food stores might stock this if unavailable elsewhere. Powdered, unflavored gelatin can be substituted.

katsuo-bushi: Dried bonito; shaved and use as a soup stock base. A convenient combination of *dashi-konbu* and *katsuo-bushi* in "teabag" form is sometimes available under the name *Dashi-no-moto*.

mirin: Sweet *saké* used for cooking. *Saké* sweetened with sugar to taste can be substituted, as can a sweet Western white wine.

miso: Bean paste; used for *miso* soup, flavorings and sauces. *Miso* comes in a spectrum of flavors and colors, from very salty to "sweet," from light beige to dark chocolate. The "sweeter" *miso* is usually best for the Western palate. The adventurous cook will find a world of interesting uses for this versatile and flavorful food.

mitsuba: Trefoil. Watercress can usually be substituted, and sometimes parsley.

nori: Thin, pressed sheets of laver. *Nori* comes in a variety of grades and types; a bit of experimentation will allow you to choose your favorite.

saké: Japanese *saké* (rice wine) should be available or can be ordered at any liquor dealer.

sansho: A Japanese spice (*anthoxylum piperitum*). Powdered *sansho* is a pleasant addition to any spice shelf. Sometimes freshly ground black pepper can be substituted.

shichimi-togarashi ("seven flavors pepper"): A blend of seasonings and spices, including ground chili pepper. A mixture of roughly ground chili, ground sesame seed, dried and ground orange or lemon peel, roughly ground black pepper, poppy seeds (and *sansho*, if available) will substitute.

shirataki: Clear vermicelli made from devil's tongue starch. Used in *sukiyaki* and Japanese one-pot cookery.

shungiku: A green, leafy vegetable of the chrysanthemum family. Parboiled young spinach, chard, or mustard greens often can be substituted; for one-pot cookery, cabbage can be used.

somen: Vermicelli. Italian-style vermicelli can be substituted.

soy sauce: The Japanese product is lighter, less salty and more versatile than the Western version. Japanese soy sauce should be available in most American supermarkets; this will prove to be a "necessary" seasoning for any kitchen.

sunomono: Vegetables and crabmeat, shrimp or fish marinated in a light vinegar mixture (e.g., *sanbai-zu* or *nihai-zu*).

wasabi: The Japanese equivalent of horseradish. Powdered *wasabi* should be available in Japanese food stores; Western horseradish is the best substitute.

yaki-dofu: Roasted *tofu*: used in *sukiyaki* and one-pot cookery.

yuzu: An aromatic citrus fruit similar to citron. Lime is a good substitute.